Coping™

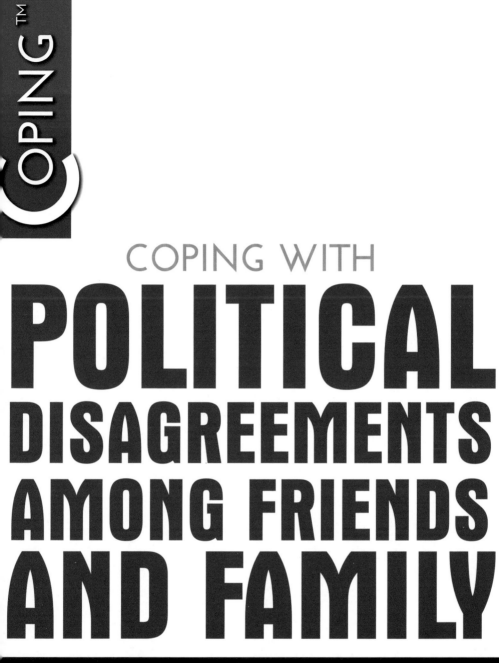

COPING WITH

POLITICAL
DISAGREEMENTS
AMONG FRIENDS
AND FAMILY

Avery Elizabeth Hurt

Rosen
YA™

New York

For all those people in my life who love me in spite of my politics

Published in 2019 by The Rosen Publishing Group, Inc.
29 East 21st Street, New York, NY 10010

Copyright © 2019 by The Rosen Publishing Group, Inc.

First Edition

Library of Congress Cataloging-in-Publication Data

Names: Hurt, Avery Elizabeth.
Title: Coping with political disagreements among friends and family / Avery Elizabeth Hurt.
Description: New York : Rosen Publishing, 2019. | Series: Coping | Includes bibliographical references and index. | Audience: Grades 7–12.
Identifiers: ISBN 9781508179085 (library bound) | ISBN 9781508179078 (pbk.)
Subjects: LCSH: Interpersonal conflict—Juvenile literature. | Conflict management—Juvenile literature. | Communication in politics—Juvenile literature. | Communication in families—Juvenile literature. | Friendship—Juvenile literature.
Classification: LCC BF723.I645 H87 2019 | DDC 303.6'9—dc23

Manufactured in the United States of America

CONTENTS

INTRODUCTION

Have you ever been in an argument with someone, maybe in the school lunchroom, and another person at the table piped up and said something like, "Hey, guys, keep it civil"? The peacemaker was probably just trying to keep you from calling each other nasty names, or worse yet, starting to throw yeast rolls at each other. When he said "keep it civil," he just meant be polite and nice to each other, and don't disturb everyone else's lunch with your bickering! But that word "civil" is pretty interesting. It comes from an old Latin word that means "citizen." Being civil means being a citizen. So how did a word that means "being a citizen" come to mean "being nice"? Well, at least in part because it can be very hard to run a society, especially a democracy, when no one can agree on anything. Expressing your views rationally and politely and being willing to listen to and consider other people's opinions is the only way for a democracy to function smoothly. But political disagreements are as important as they are inevitable. If everyone always saw things the same way, we'd never have any new ideas and never make any progress.

"We the People" are a diverse and varied bunch. The 2016 US presidential election clearly showed that the country was pretty much evenly split between "the left" and "the right." (The vote was split almost in half,

Having political arguments with your friends doesn't have to be a bad thing—you just have to keep it civil.

with Donald Trump winning the Electoral College, and Hillary Clinton winning the popular vote.) In the past, even if a society was diverse, families were generally pretty homogeneous. But these days, Trump voters share Thanksgiving dinner with Clinton supporters. Pro-life activists are married to pro-choice advocates. Best friends take opposing stands on gun control. Gay couples are surprised to discover that some of the people on their wedding invitation list aren't so keen on gay marriage.

The trick is, as the guy in the lunchroom said, to "keep it civil."

That may not be hard to do when you disagree with a stranger. After all, you can just walk away if things get too sticky. But what about when the person you disagree with is your best bud? Or a member of your family? Maybe even your parents? When you have political disagreements with the people who matter most to you, you have to figure out a way to disagree and still get along. You're probably eager to share your thoughts and opinions with the people closest to you. It's also important to hear what people who disagree with you have to say. You'll probably learn a lot more than you expect. But if want to share and learn without harming loved ones or your relationships with them, you need to know how to disagree in a kind, productive way—how to keep it civil. Political disagreements are inevitable these days, even with family. But this book will show you how to keep yours healthy, safe, and believe it or not, useful.

At Home

People have been arguing about politics since the ancient Greeks invented democracy— probably a lot longer than that. In the Bible, there is a story about people asking Jesus to settle a debate about whether they should pay taxes. Friendships have been ruined and families torn apart when people who truly loved one another were unable to get beyond their political disagreements.

Sometimes, it seems like things are just getting worse. For a lot of people these days, just opening their Facebook page is an exercise in conflict management. Some people actually do homework and practice their lines before a family gathering so that they can be prepared to respond to the outrageous things they know their relatives are going to say. It can be tempting just to avoid people you disagree with. That's not a very practical solution, though. You don't want to avoid your family, even if sometimes you might think you do. And you certainly don't want to lose your friends.

Friends talk about all kinds of topics. Many of them aren't areas of controversy, but those that are don't have to ruin friendships.

Some people deal with the problem by limiting all their conversations to "safe" subjects. We can talk about the weather, what we're having for dinner, and Aunt June's eye-popping new hair color. Maybe if we're an exceptionally good-natured group, we can discuss sports. But we can't talk about politics without fighting, so we just don't go there.

That approach might work— at least, it might keep everyone from being at each other's throats. And for some families and groups of friends, it might be the only solution. But there are a couple of reasons it's not the best approach. For one thing, if you have conversations only with people who think the same way you do, you'll never learn anything. As hard as it may be to believe if you've just been reading your social media news feed, the people you disagree with often have a lot to teach you. (It's just best to have those conversations in person and using more than 280 characters.)

That doesn't mean these people will change your mind, though they might. It just means that they will give you many different ways of thinking about important issues. It's also useful to understand why people believe the things they believe. You need to know this if you are hoping to change their minds, of course. But you also need to know this if you are trying to figure out how to live comfortably and peacefully with them even if you can't change their minds.

So how do you pull that off?

Common Ground

Often, it turns out that people's views aren't as different as they seem at first glance. The political climate in the United States today seems dangerously polarized. Sometimes, it seems as if half the country believes one thing, while the other half believes exactly the opposite. And there's not an inch of middle ground in between. But when you take a closer look, you'll find that things are not quite as extreme as that. Take gun control, for example. Now that's an issue that gets people stirred up. Some people are for it. Some are against it. Some think it's absolutely necessary to have gun control to reduce the number of innocent people who die from gun violence every year. Others think gun control is just a way to take people's guns away so that they can't protect themselves.

But polls show that when you get down to the specifics, people aren't quite as polarized as it seems. Almost all voters in the United States believe that there should be background checks on people who buy guns, so that we can prevent criminals from buying them. Almost no one in the United States advocates completely "taking people's guns away." When two people from opposing sides of the gun control debate sit down to discuss the issue, they often find that they don't disagree on as much as they thought. And where they do disagree, there's room for discussion. This is true of most issues. But how would you ever know that if you didn't talk with and listen to people you disagreed with? The question is, how do you have a civilized discussion in the first place? How do you keep honest political disagreements from turning into long-term feuds that can ruin relationships? How do you keep from saying things that you will regret for years?

One way is to lose the notion of right and wrong. In most disagreements, what's right and what's wrong is not all that clear. Someone might be wrong about some of her facts, but that's not the same as being wrong about her positions or her beliefs. If you find the common ground—for example, you both want to keep your families safe—then the discussion can focus on different ways to achieve what you both want. That way, even if you disagree about the details, you're on the same team.

Nothing New

It's hard to imagine a political campaign more brutal than the 2016 US presidential election. But the election of 1800 may have been almost as bad. Thomas Jefferson and John Adams, two of the people most responsible for founding the United States, were in a tight race for the presidency. Adams was president and was being challenged for reelection by Jefferson, his vice president.

Both candidates thought the fate of the nation was at stake. On the one hand, Jefferson believed that Adams had put too much power in the central government. He was convinced that if such a pattern continued, the voice of the people, especially minorities, would not be heard. On the other hand, Adams feared Jefferson's support for the common people would lead to civil unrest, even bloodshed.

It was a nasty campaign. In those days, candidates didn't give speeches on the campaign trail, much less hold rallies. They were much too dignified for that. Both men had written extensively about their views of government. Curious voters were welcome to investigate and make their decision. The press, however, was another matter. Early American newspapers were extremely partisan. Writers on both sides took up their pens and composed vicious attacks on the candidate they opposed. Jefferson was accused of engaging in vivisection and bizarre rituals at his Virginia home. Adams was accused of plotting to have his daughter marry one of the sons of King George so that he could establish a British dynasty in the United States. None of this was remotely true. Sound familiar? In the end, Jefferson won, but he won by a very narrow margin.

R-E-S-P-E-C-T

When it comes to political disagreements with friends and family, you have to keep one thing in mind. You love these people, and they love you.

That doesn't always mean you always like them, of course. Sometimes, you might feel like pulling your hair out. Sometimes, you are convinced that the people you are sharing your life with are a bunch of dunderheads, and maybe obnoxious dunderheads at that. But remember that you love them. Try to show a little respect. Of course, it can be extremely hard to respect people you truly believe are just plain wrong. If they are really nasty when they express their opinions, it can be even harder to respect them. But you might be amazed at what happens if you really try to be respectful (even if you have to fake it a little bit at first).

You can get very angry with a sibling or other family member and still love him or her very much. Keep your argument skills in mind so that things don't blow up.

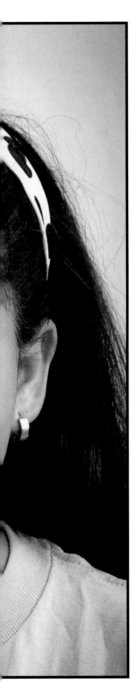

It's not as hard as it seems, either. Here are a few argument skills that can be very helpful when you respectfully disagree:

- **Stay calm** (even if the other person isn't). A shouting match is not an argument, and it's certainly not a discussion. And oddly, if you become very calm, the other person often does, too. Rather than trying to match each increase in volume, try going the other way. As you become calmer and more soft-spoken, the person you are talking to will calm down, too. If he doesn't, he might risk looking like a nut job.

- **Ask questions.** People want to be heard—that's why they keep shouting at you. If someone says something you disagree with, you can reply by stating your own opinion. But if both people are convinced they are right, the conversation isn't going anywhere. Instead, ask for specifics. "Why do you think that?" "What's the recent data on this?" Just make sure your questions aren't confrontational. There's a world of difference between saying, "I'd love to see some data on how much tropical storms have increased in recent years," and saying, "What makes you actually believe that climate change is making hurricanes worse?"

- **Listen.** One of the best things you can do in an argument is to listen. You might learn something from the person you are disagreeing with. But not only that; being a good listener makes the people you're arguing with feel respected. If you listen to them, they are more likely to listen to you in turn. That makes it so much easier to find common ground. And, even if you don't, it will make it much easier to stay friends and have a happy home life.

- **Use "I" statements.** It's easy for arguments to turn personal. "You're just a snowflake!" "Don't be such an old fossil."

Learning how to listen well is just as important as learning how to communicate well. Many of us need practice.

"Only an idiot would think ..." People can go on the defensive even if you aren't being quite that confrontational. Most people want to be right, so when you disagree with them, they get defensive and double down on their own position. If you seem to be getting the better of them in the debate, they might even get personal. You can reduce the chances of this happening by simply changing the way you express things. Instead of saying, "You're not making sense," say, "I'm having trouble following your logic." Or instead of saying, "You don't have the facts that back up that statement," try saying, "I'd love to see some more facts to back that up." (Of course, you mustn't sneer or sound superior when you say this, or the effort will be totally lost.)

- **Be kind.** Never, ever make another person look or feel stupid (even if you are momentarily convinced that he or she is). It's a cruel thing to do, and when we slip up and do it, we almost always regret it. One of the best ways to turn a temporary disagreement into a lifelong rift is by putting someone down and making that person feel stupid. Never forget the essential humanity of the person you are disagreeing with. That person may be confused. Or misinformed. He or she may be just plain wrong. But he or she is still a human being.

Is This an Argument or Not?

We use the word "argument" in two similar but slightly different ways. If you and your parents are having an energetic exchange of words about who gets to use to car this weekend, you might call that a quarrel or a squabble. Or you might even call it an argument. However, there is another meaning of the word "argument," and it doesn't (usually) have much to do with people yelling at each other. That sense of "argument" means to make a carefully thought-out—or argued—defense of your position. Lawyers present arguments to judges. Philosophers make arguments to support their positions. Candidates make arguments about why you should vote for them. If you can make that kind of argument carefully enough, you might avoid getting into the other kind of argument.

Respect Yourself

As important as it is to respect the people you disagree with, it is just as important to respect yourself. You should also expect others to respect you. You can

You don't have to be pushy and arrogant to have self-respect, and respecting yourself will encourage others to respect you, too.

keep conflicts from getting out of hand by being a good listener, staying calm, and being willing to find common ground. But that doesn't mean you have to give in on every point. If you've done your homework, gathered your support, and carefully thought through your opinions, then you can and should feel comfortable expressing them. Just be sure to extend to other people the same respect you expect them to give you.

The next few chapters talk about how to use these techniques, and some others, to cope with political disagreements wherever you are: at school, at church, in your community, or online.

CHAPTER TWO

At School

School can be one of the places you're most likely to have problems with political disagreements. If you go to a large enough school, you'll almost certainly meet people from all across the political spectrum—and you're likely to become friends with people all across the political spectrum. If you go to a small school, perhaps in a small town, you may have the opposite problem: everyone thinks alike. That might feel nice and cozy, for a while. But if you begin to disagree with some of the basic positions of your community, then it might be even trickier to talk about this with your classmates.

Conversely, school can be one of the best places for working out those disagreements in a friendly way. There is absolutely no reason to lose friends over political issues. You don't have to change their minds, and they don't have to change yours. Instead, you can learn from each other. After all, learning is what school is all about.

It's easy to think of politics like it's a team sport. But pitting one party against another is a dangerous attitude.

It's Not Just Blue and Red

One of the most exciting things about school can be rooting for the sports teams. In today's polarized political environment, it's easy to think of politics as sport. The Democrats are blue, and the Republicans are red. The Republicans have an elephant mascot. The

Democrats have a donkey. You pick the team—liberal or conservative—that roughly matches your values. Then you support that team no matter what. You don't have to give it much thought. Your "team" is always right, and even if they aren't, they're better than the other team. We have elections. One party wins and the other loses. The morning after an election your candidate won, you feel that relieved, happy feeling you get after your school's team has won a big championship.

Politics is very different from sports, though. When you choose a candidate to support, you are choosing a leader who will be one of the people to make important decisions about your town, your state, or your nation. This is a lot more important than which team takes home the pennant.

There's an even more important reason elections aren't like sporting events and political parties aren't like teams. Once an election is over and the winners have been chosen, everyone sits down together and decides how to go about running the city, state, or national government. In a democracy, no matter what individual or what party wins an election, everyone keeps working together to govern society. At least that's how democracy works when it's functioning properly, which is why the sports analogy for politics doesn't quite work. There's a much better one.

Come Join Us

It's not always as exciting, and you don't have team colors and clever mascots, but the place where school is similar to politics is in … surprise … school politics. That doesn't mean just student government. That means all sorts of school groups and organizations. It's groups like the Key Club, Future Business Leaders, the Christian Union Group, Gay-Straight Alliance clubs, the Drama Club, the Science Club, and dozens more. Students who are involved in these groups are by definition school leaders. As school leaders, they have an enormous opportunity to set the tone of the school's discourse. Getting involved in one or more school groups gives you a chance to deal with political disagreements at school in a civil and productive way. And it gives you a chance to help other people do the same.

If this approach is going to work, however, you have to avoid one big pitfall of organizations. Joining a group can be a way of avoiding people with conflicting views. If you just hang out with the kids who think the way you do, you won't get a chance to develop skills for dealing with political disagreements or for helping your school develop a more civil political environment. That's not a big problem in a group that attracts people from all points on the political spectrum. You'll probably meet all kinds of people in the drama club or the business club. But a gay-straight alliance club is likely to be made up mostly of people who are progressive on lesbian, gay, bisexual, transgender, and queer (LGBTQ) issues. The science club is not likely to have too many members who think climate change is a hoax. That's why you need to pitch a big tent. For example, the purpose of gay-straight alliance groups is to help people, both gay and straight, learn about the issues facing the LGBTQ community. Obviously, people who are sympathetic to these issues will be inclined to attend meetings and events sponsored by the club. But if you reach out to those who are not so sympathetic, you'll get a chance to have discussions with people who have different views. You can learn what they have to say, and they can hear what you have to say. Christian student organizations have a similar opportunity. Christian groups often spend a lot of time and effort trying to convert new members. That's fine. But it might be helpful to simply open their meetings and activities to non-Christians with the intent of opening a dialogue.

This does not mean that you have to change your views. Not at all. The purpose of getting together people of widely different views is not to change your own views, any more than it is to change theirs. It is to learn how to communicate with people who have different views. The populations of Canada and the United States are becoming increasingly diverse, both

When people from different religions welcome each other into their lives, members of each faith can learn from members of the other, and friendships are made.

ethnically and in terms of political views and beliefs. For democracy in those nations to remain strong, people must learn to work together in spite of their differences. You can help make this happen by starting with your school organizations.

Talking sticks are just one way to make sure everyone gets a fair chance to have a say—without worrying about interruptions.

Say What?

It's easy enough to send out the invitations. But what do you do when all these different people actually show up in the tent? How do you talk and listen to others when you're coming from such vastly different places? Many of the techniques mentioned in chapter 1 are useful here: stay calm, listen, use "I" statements, and be kind. But when you are a school leader, there is a lot more you can do.

For one thing, you have a say in the rules of the organization. Ground rules that prohibit offensive, insulting, or bullying talk will set the tone for the conversations. Also, it's useful to have some kind of system for making sure anyone who wants to talk gets a chance to do so. For an informal meeting or event, you might try a talking stick. Whoever has the stick gets to talk. No one is allowed to interrupt. When that person has had her say, the stick is passed to the next person. More formal meetings can have speakers who represent a variety of views. It's also a good idea to put some of the calmest, most easygoing people in your group in charge of these events. They will set the tone. More often than not, if an event is set up and led in a kind and respectful way, the people who attend will follow suit. If you're having trouble keeping control of the meeting or event, ask a teacher or other adult to intervene.

Doing a little homework can help you understand and appreciate the views of others. That doesn't mean you have to agree, of course.

Good preparation can help ensure the success of the big-tent approach. Do your homework (and make sure everyone else also has a chance to do so). Read up on the views, values, and issues that matter to the people you don't agree with. Don't let this get you worked up! It's not an opportunity to practice demolishing their arguments. It's a chance to develop some understanding, even if you don't agree. Ask yourself why a person might have these views. Why does this matter so much to this person? Even if you think he is totally, absolutely, irredeemably wrong, you can still develop some sympathy for his views.

It's also a good idea to open and close the event or meeting with something totally unrelated to the controversial issue. Encourage people to just visit and talk and get to know one another. (This might be a good time for conversations about sports!) Then, when you settle down to talk about serious issues, everyone will remember that they're talking with friends, not opponents. Or at least that's the tone you're trying to set. It may take some time, but chances are good that you'll get there. Be sure to close the meeting with some warm, friendly, inclusive messages, too. That will make people feel as welcomed when they leave as they did when they arrived.

Facts Matter

All too often, what are intended to be calm, reasonable discussions of political matters turn into verbal brawls. People spout their opinions, and others counter with theirs. If it never gets beyond this, you aren't having a political discussion. You aren't even having a political dispute. You're just having a shouting match. In order for it to be a political discussion, you have to deal with facts. There are good ways and bad ways of asking people to support their opinions with facts, but if the conversation is going to be civilized and productive, you have to deal with facts. The best way to keep a political conversation fact centered is to set a good example. Do some homework, and know your stuff.

Be sure that you get your information from reliable sources. It can be very comforting to visit websites and read opinion pieces by people you already agree with. And many times, these people know what they're talking about. But be careful. When you already have an opinion on a topic, it can be hard to look without bias at information that supports that opinion. Try to find data from neutral sources. For example, if you're looking for data on how many immigrants commit crimes, check government (national or local) crime statistics databases. Gather facts not just on your position but on your opponents' positions as well. Whatever you do, don't just throw

Sharing your research will help others in your organization be as well prepared as you are when it comes time to discuss controversial issues.

around numbers you've seen on social media. Social media will be discussed in a later chapter, but for now, just remember that you have to be very careful about information you get that way.

Once you've collected the data, have it available at the meeting. You might print handouts for a meeting. But even if the event is too informal for that, be sure you are thoroughly acquainted with the facts of the issue—facts that support your position as well as facts that challenge it. Remember what you are aiming for is a discussion, not a lecture.

Your school probably has a lot of resources to help you with this project. When studying the issues, enlist the help of teachers and librarians. Joining the debate club and taking a rhetoric class are great ways to hone your skills at discussing controversial matters.

Myths & FACTS

Myth: Religious organizations aren't allowed in schools.

Fact: It's true that public schools cannot promote religion. However, as long as schools treat all groups equally, they can allow religion-based groups to form and meet on school property. The group must be student initiated and student led, and participation must be voluntary.

Myth: It's impossible to be friends with someone who has a vastly different worldview.

Fact: In today's political climate, it may sometimes seem that way. But the fact is, some very rewarding friendships are between people who disagree on political issues. Ulysses S. Grant, the US general who helped bring an end to the Civil War, was good friends with James Longstreet, a general in the Confederate army. Their friendship survived the war. Since leaving office, former presidents Bill Clinton and George H. W. Bush have become quite good friends as they work together on humanitarian projects. Liberal senator Ted

(continued on the next page)

(continued from the previous page)

Kennedy and conservative senator Orrin Hatch were good friends until Kennedy's death in 2009. They worked across party lines to pass an insurance program for children. The list of people who refused to let politics ruin friendship is long.

Myth: Schools are isolated and protected environments, nothing like the real world.

Fact: Schools are in many ways small versions of the larger society. There is no better place for young people to hone their skills in working with others and helping improve their world than in their own schools.

Family Matters

When you get home from school, political discussions are a totally different kind of experience. In some families, everyone agrees on politics. When the subject comes up, people just share news they've heard that day. They might groan about a resolution passed by the city council, or they might cheer a recent Supreme Court ruling. But they don't get into disagreements or debates. Most families aren't like this, though. Even if they agree generally on most things, there are often points of conflict when it comes to politics. That doesn't have to tear a family apart. It doesn't even have to ruin family dinners or long car trips. It can actually make life richer and relationships deeper. But it does take a bit of effort.

Unbroken Homes

You might think married couples would share political views. After all, why would someone marry a person who disagreed with him or her on such basic issues as how the nation should be governed? However, a 2016 study found that only 55 percent of married couples in the United States belonged to the same political party. We can't know what dinnertime is like for the other 45 percent, but we do know mixed-political marriages can work. Even people who care very deeply about politics can overcome their differences. Mary Matalin and James Carville are one such couple, though they are an extreme example. Matalin and Carville have very different political views. In fact, they are almost total opposites when it comes to politics. On top of that, they are both political analysts who've worked in national political campaigns. They've been advisors to presidents and presidential candidates. Politics for these two is not a just a topic of conversation. It's serious business. So how do they live together without throwing the crockery? In an interview with *U.S. News & World Report,* Matalin said that she and Carville both strongly believed in "the need for informed citizenry and participatory democracy." This belief is what keeps their differences from

Mary Matalin and James Carville are seen here at the reopening of the Orpheum Theatre in New Orleans, Louisiana. Despite their differing political opinions, they enjoy each other's company.

pulling them apart. Matalin also said it comes down to this: "We love each other." Families—people who love each other—find ways to work through disagreements, whether those are about whose turn it is to wash the dishes or who should be the leader of the nation.

Another study, this one published in December 2015, found that about half of US kids shared their parents' political beliefs. (It's worth noting that a fair number of kids didn't even know their parents' political beliefs. Perhaps those families don't have political discussions at the dinner table.) This study also found that family political discussions help kids refine and develop their own political positions. This is the case whether kids agree or disagree with their parents. So talking about politics is helpful. You just have to do it in a way that doesn't create hostility. And just like at school, it can be done. But at home, it takes a very different strategy. (Hint: you won't need to print out information sheets.)

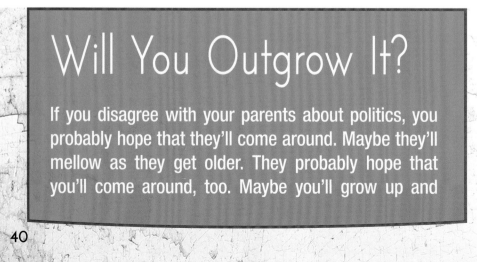

Will You Outgrow It?

If you disagree with your parents about politics, you probably hope that they'll come around. Maybe they'll mellow as they get older. They probably hope that you'll come around, too. Maybe you'll grow up and get wiser. In a poem called "Precaution," Robert Frost wrote, "I never dared be radical when young / For fear it would make me conservative when old." Is it true that people's political beliefs change as they age? And if so, do those changes follow any pattern? Are older people more conservative than younger ones?

A 2014 study by the Pew Research Center examined the political beliefs of different age groups. The study found that older people were pretty evenly spread on a left-to-right spectrum. About a third of the older people surveyed were to the left of the political spectrum. A third were to the right. And the rest were somewhere in the middle. The pattern for young people was similar. So Robert Frost may have gotten that wrong. Older people aren't necessarily more conservative than younger ones. The details mattered, though. The Pew study found that no matter how conservative they were on economic issues, young people were far more liberal on social issues, such as gay rights and immigration, than older folks. Another study suggests that Frost was also wrong about changing as we age. It found that people's views don't change dramatically after they are grown. So, if your parents are hoping you'll outgrow your beliefs, they may be disappointed. And you might not want to count on your parents mellowing out either. The best strategy is probably just to learn to get along despite your differences.

Pul-eez, Mom ...

Chapter 1 discussed being respectful of your opponent when you are having political disagreements. That is even more important when the opponent is your parent. And oddly, it can sometimes be even more difficult. When you disagree with people you care deeply about, you want them to have what you believe are "the right" views. You don't want your parents to be old people who just don't get it. And you don't want them embarrassing you with their bumper stickers. Your parents probably have similar feelings about you and your opinions. They don't want you to grow up to be some kind of bozo who believes all the wrong things! And they don't want their friends thinking they don't know how to raise sensible children. Often, within families, there is more at stake than just how many votes your favorite candidate is likely to get.

It can be helpful to stop occasionally and remind yourself of the things your parents get right. You might think they are totally wrongheaded about politics, but they probably do a pretty good job of keeping you fed and housed. That doesn't mean they are always right. It does mean that they just might be worth listening to. The first chapter gave an overview of some techniques for showing respect for people you disagree with. Here are a few additional tips for when those people just happen to be your parents:

Although political disagreements with your parents can be especially difficult, it's well worth the effort to get beyond those differences.

- **Admit that you may change your mind one day.** More than anyone, parents know you are a work in progress. Growing up is all about figuring things out. Your parents will probably be a lot more comfortable with your views if you make it clear that those views aren't written in stone. You may not change your mind. Ever. But the important thing is realizing and admitting that one day, you might.

- **Listen.** This is even more important with your parents than with other people. Their job is to teach you and keep you safe. If you aren't at least listening and considering what they have to say, their job is almost impossible. Try to give them a break on this. If you do, they'll probably be much more likely to listen to what you have to say.

- **Realize that *they* might change their minds.** It might not be a good idea to point this out, but your parents may change their minds, too. Plenty of grown children have been happily shocked to find out that their parents didn't disapprove of their adult lifestyles as much as they expected them to. Times change, and people change with them—even older people. They might not change their basic political stance, but there is an excellent chance that they'll become more accepting of you. Your parents are far more interested in your happiness than your political views. Once they know that you're doing just fine, they'll be far less concerned with how you vote.

But what if the problem is that your parents don't respect you? You might try asking them for respect. You could say something like, "Mom and Dad, I know you don't agree with me. And I know that I am still young and still trying to figure things out. But it would help me a lot if you could respect my views. We can disagree, and you can tell me why you think I'm wrong. But I'll probably learn a lot more if you do it with respect." This only works, though, if you respect your parents, too. In fact, you might be able to set an example for how to disagree and stay civil.

Political disagreements with siblings can be even worse than disagreements with parents. You're probably not in the habit of being respectful to your sibs (or they to you). Lots of people have found that after they get older, they get closer to their sibs, even if their political views are still at odds. You don't have to wait until you are older. Having political discussions with a brother or sister might help you hone your techniques. It might also bring you closer to your siblings. Use the same ground rules you use for talking with other people—and insist your sibs do, too.

Vietnam

The Vietnam War was one of the most difficult periods in American history. On the one hand, people who supported the war believed that if the United States did not win the war in Vietnam, Soviet-backed Communists would take over all of Asia. They might even take over North and South America, too. On the other hand, people who opposed the war felt like American young people were dying for a lost cause. They said that America could not win the Vietnam War. They pointed out that losing it would not be as catastrophic as many people believed. Because young men were being drafted to fight in Vietnam, many young people opposed the war. Older people, perhaps remembering World War II, were more likely to support it. Debates about the war caused serious damage to many families.

In 2017, more than forty years after the war ended, filmmakers Ken Burns and Lynn Novick released a television series about Vietnam. Just before the series aired, Burns and Novick showed clips of the film at the Kennedy Center in Washington, DC. Before the screening, Burns asked audience members who had served in the war to stand. The audience gave the veterans a warm ovation. Then he asked members of the audience who had protested the war to stand. Again, the audience, including the veterans who had just stood, gave a warm and respectful applause to the protestors. Forty years is a long time. But the wounds of Vietnam have begun to heal. Maybe knowing that will help today's wounds heal more quickly.

(Not So) Happy Holidays

Many a Thanksgiving dinner has been totally ruined by political arguments. Most families have at least one hothead who can't stop serving up political views along with the stuffing. That doesn't mean you have to skip out on the festivities. There's rarely much to be gained by getting into political discussions with people you see only a few times a year. If politics can be avoided over the turkey, that's probably best. If not, try to keep things as calm as you can. When others get confrontational, don't take the bait. If someone says something particularly infuriating (or flat-out wrong), just let it pass. If someone insults another member of your family or an ethnic group, you may need to speak up. But you can do it gently. "I realize you feel strongly about immigration, Uncle Dick, but we all love Hamid." Then change the subject. "Aunt Louise, this casserole is outstanding!" If you're the target, you might say something like, "It's Thanksgiving. I'm not in the mood to argue. Let's just enjoy being together." You don't have to point out every wrong statement or call people out on every unkindness. Life-and-

death decisions are rarely made over holiday dinners. Sometimes, it's best just to let things go.

Whether it's a holiday or not, the most difficult conflicts to deal with are often those you aren't really involved in. Watching your parents argue, or your parents and a sibling get into it, can be tough. You may not even care about the issue. But you care very much about the people who are in conflict.

Often, conflicts get out of hand because people misunderstand one another. You might be able to help by saying something like, "I don't think Dad meant that everyone who supported Donald Trump is a racist, just that some of his voters might

Family dinners can be a great time for good conversation and bonding. They can also be the place for distressing arguments.

Often the best thing you can do when friends are disagreeing is step in and help them see each other's point of view.

be." Or you might ask questions that need to be asked, but the people arguing aren't asking. "Jane, do you think there's any way to make sure potential terrorists can't get guns without violating the Second Amendment?" And if nothing else seems to be working, you can always suggest a group hug.

The important thing to remember is that political issues come and go. But we always have our families. It's worth a little patience and compromise to keep our families happy.

CHAPTER FOUR

Among Friends

I t may seem surprising, but it can often be harder to disagree with your friends than with your parents.

When you are a little kid, you depend on your parents for everything. Most little kids think their parents are almost superheroes. When you start to get older, it's time to start, very gradually, developing a little independence. You walk to and from school by yourself. Maybe you stay at home alone after school until your parents get home from work. You take more responsibility— you might help plan and cook meals or do the shopping. Maybe you help care for younger kids in your family. You make more decisions on your own, without having to check in with your parents about every little thing. And your parents don't wear their superhero capes quite so often. You still love your parents—and they are probably still

At some point in life, disagreements with friends can start to come up more often—and they can be very distressing.

heroes to you. But you begin to notice that sometimes they make mistakes, and sometimes they're wrong. This is the time when you are trying to figure out who you are, not just as a part of your family, but as a part of the larger world. You are becoming more of an individual and less an extension of mom and dad.

At the same time that your parents are having a little bit less influence on you, your friends start to have more. That's natural, too. When your world begins to extend beyond your family, it naturally extends to your friends. At that point in life, it can seem very important to be accepted by your friends. Disagreeing with them can be upsetting. And these days, those disagreements are often about politics.

Danger Zone

Political issues are important. But they are rarely as important as friendships. There may be times when it is better to give up a friendship than to compromise your political values. Those times don't happen often, though. If you have a friend whose political beliefs are so different from yours that you can't even talk about politics without getting angry, it might be better just to make politics off limits. You can still hang out. You can play ball or video games and talk about school or sports. You can go shopping or watch a movie. You just don't talk about politics. It's not that hard to do.

It may be easier than you think to enjoy life with your friends without spending any time at all discussing politics.

There's a lot to life besides politics. In fact, it's that life besides politics that makes politics important. The issues we are passionate about—the things we're arguing about—are the decisions about how to run and live in our world. And we decide how best to do that by having ordinary lives, schools, jobs, activities … friends. Without those, what would be the purpose of government? Why would we care about politics?

It's not hard to set limits on political talk. You could have a hand signal or code word that you use whenever politics tries to creep into a conversation. The code word doesn't have to mean anything, just so you both know it's your reminder to stop talking about things that could create conflict. "Danger zone" or "trouble ahead" might work. Anything would do, as long as you both know what it means. If it's a word that has special meaning for you and your friends, that's even better.

Talking politics with friends, however, is a great way to get a better idea of the issues and where you stand on them. If you talk only with people you agree with, then you're living in a pretty small world. If the people you disagree with are your friends, it's much easier to listen to them and give their views a fair hearing. One of the biggest advantages to having political disagreements with friends is that you learn that people can disagree and still get along. The world is full of many different kinds of people with many different worldviews. And we all have to share the world. If we learn to do this with civility and kindness, the world will be a much better place.

In and Out of Chambers

Ruth Bader Ginsburg has been one of the most consistently liberal Supreme Court justices in recent times. Antonin Scalia was one of the most reliably conservative. Until Scalia's death in 2016, the two were dear friends. They had fundamental disagreements about the general nature of government and the interpretation of the US Constitution. They also disagreed on the particulars. Scalia was adamantly opposed to LGBTQ rights. Ginsburg was the first Supreme Court justice to officiate a same-sex marriage. Scalia voted to gut legislation that protected voting rights in districts with a history of voter suppression. Ginsburg wrote a scathing dissent of that opinion. Neither was known for mincing words on or off the bench. Scalia could be outlandish and arrogant. Ginsburg is quieter, even a bit shy, but she has a quick wit and doesn't

(continued on the next page)

Supreme Court justices Ruth Bader Ginsburg and Antonin Scalia, seen here during a portrait session at the Supreme Court, were very different but also very dear friends.

(continued from the previous page)

hesitate to express her opinions. All the same, the two were congenial colleagues.

The friendship between Ginsburg and Scalia went beyond work. They shared many interests—opera, good food, and a sense of fun. Their families regularly shared meals and spent New Year's Eve together. After Scalia's death, Ginsburg wrote, "We were best buddies." Ginsburg said that their friendship was a demonstration that respectful debate made the Supreme Court stronger. This can be a lesson to the rest of the nation. No matter how polarized we become, no matter how strongly we disagree, we can still be respectful. We can even be best buddies.

Staying Friends

One way to keep things friendly even when you disagree is to talk about civics rather than politics. After the 2016 US presidential election, a lot of people were talking about how Trump won the election but Clinton won the popular vote. That discussion often got mired in just how many people voted for each candidate and where each candidate's voters lived. And that, of course, quickly led to often unfriendly political discussions. But if you try, you can steer discussions into safer territory. It's often more interesting territory as well. No matter who you wanted to win the election, you can't help being fascinated by the complex way the US election system works. Why the electoral college? Why the two-party system? How often has

Political arguments can often distract us from far more interesting—and productive—discussions, where there may be more common ground than we thought.

the candidate with the fewest popular votes won the presidency? In the election of 1800, the House of Representatives chose the president. How did that work? Could that happen again? Even though we have many different views about politics, most of us are big fans of democracy. Talking about the best way to make democracy work offers opportunities for plenty of fascinating discussions that get beyond any particular candidate or policy proposal. And if the discussion does get back around to topics you disagree on, you've already found a lot of common ground.

When you do get into disagreements with friends, it can be very tempting to try to change their minds. After all, you like these people, and they are so wrong! You just want to straighten them out! That's understandable, but it's also tricky. For one thing, right and wrong aren't always so clear-cut—especially in politics. Even when you're absolutely convinced on general matters (everyone should have the right to vote), you can still not be sure about the details (how old should a person be before being allowed to vote?). It might not be a great idea to try to change your friends' minds until you're sure you've made up yours. Also, keep in mind that just like you, your friends are still trying to work out who they are and what they believe. If you start trying to convert your friends to your way of thinking, you might put more pressure on them than they need right now. The best thing to do is to make your point as clearly and logically as you can. Then listen to what your friends have to say.

When It's Time to Stand Your Ground

Earlier, we talked about how friendships are more important than politics. And most of the time, that's true. There are times, though, when you might have to give up a friendship because of different political beliefs. Friendships don't have to end because one person supports more government involvement in the economy than the other. There's no reason to let positions on foreign policy or environmental regulations ruin a friendship. Republicans and Democrats (and Libertarians and Social Democrats) can be great friends while still having vastly different political beliefs. But when people's political beliefs and the way they express those beliefs cause harm to someone else, you have to stand up for the person being harmed, even if it means losing a friend. (Thankfully, it may not always mean that!) When your friends' political attitudes veer over into hatred and xenophobia, you may have to take a stand. You should never counter hate with hate. But you should be willing to state your beliefs firmly and without waffling. You might have to say something like, "Hey, John. You're a good friend,

Do it as kindly as you possibly can, but always try to keep a no-tolerance approach to hate, bullying, and violence.

but it really bothers me when you say those mean things about other people. Could you knock it off?" If your friend refuses, you may have to find other people to hang out with. If your friends bully or intimidate others or threaten anyone, then you need to tell your teachers or parents. Sometimes, kids repeat nasty stuff they've heard on television. They may be trying to get a response from you. Or they may not realize just how hurtful their comments are. If you kindly but firmly refuse to put up with that kind of thing, they may rethink their attitude. Political beliefs all across the spectrum are fine. Bullying, harassing, or harming other people are not.

10 Great Questions
for a Political Expert

1. My friends and I love to talk politics. But some of them just don't get their facts right. How can I correct someone without offending him or her?

2. Most of the kids I know spend a lot of time on Facebook and Instagram. They think that memes are a great way to debate politics. I think this is utterly stupid, but I don't know what to do about it. Should I just keep my mouth shut? Or is there a way to help elevate the conversation?

3. When my friends start talking about politics, I always feel left out. I have opinions, but I'm not good at expressing them. Is there a way I can get braver about expressing myself?

4. My parents are a "mixed marriage" when it comes to politics. Sometimes, I worry when they start arguing. They yell and scream and call each other names. After the argument, they seem fine again. Still, I worry they might get a divorce all because of politics. Is there anything I can do?

5. I love to study government and civics. But I hate to talk about politics. Is there an easy way to steer

(continued on the next page)

(continued from the previous page)

political discussions back to something that's still interesting but less confrontational?

6. I'm very interested in politics and want to run for office when I am older. My parents tell me I'm way too young to have opinions on such important matters. I disagree. Is there a way I can get them to understand how serious I am and to listen to me?

7. The teachers in our school often bring politics into the classroom. We have mock elections and debates. But I feel kind of outnumbered. Most of the other students have very different views than I do. I want to take part, but I feel like they'll just make fun of me. How should I handle these feelings?

8. I HATE politics. I don't want to talk about it. I don't want to hear about it. But everyone keeps telling me that I am a bad citizen if I don't keep up with politics. Is that true? Can I still be a citizen but just take a pass on the politics?

9. Everyone I know talks about politics like it's just some kind of game—like a reality show on television. But I'm honestly frightened. I'm worried about what the world is going to be like when I'm grown. Is there anything a kid can do besides talk?

10. I'd like to be better informed. What's the best way to do that? I hear so much about "fake news" that I have no idea whom to trust. Where can I turn for reliable political information?

At Church and in the Community

Often, political disagreements are about national issues. Which candidate would make the best president? What party should have the most seats in Parliament? Should the government approve an oil pipeline or a nuclear arms reduction treaty? As much attention as national politics gets, that's only part of the story. Politics begins at the local level, and political issues are closest to home when you're close to home.

"All Politics Is Local"

Many years ago, a US senator from Massachusetts said, "All politics is local." What he meant by this is that people vote based on the issues that concern them most in their daily lives. Issues such as whether the factory where they work will continue to operate or who serves on the local school board are very often more important than national issues. These days that doesn't quite ring true. Many people vote almost exclusively based on one or two big national issues. In the 2016 US presidential election, many people voted for Donald Trump primarily because they expected him to appoint a conservative justice to the US Supreme Court. (He did.) These days, national issues can have a powerful impact close to home. How a candidate stands on LGBTQ rights or what a party's plan is for health care can have an immediate impact on communities and families. Some people even support local candidates based on their positions on national issues.

It is very important to be informed about and involved with national politics. But it is just as important, if not more so, to be informed and involved with what's going on in your city and state. While all our attention is focused on national politics, we often neglect local matters. Yet local issues have the most immediate effect on our lives. Decisions made by the local school board determine when and where you will go to school. Local governments are responsible for fire and police departments. Decisions made by the city council affect regulations and taxes for local businesses. The rules and upkeep of streets and parks are managed locally. State legislatures make a lot of decisions about what subjects you will be required to study in school

Local politics have a profound effect on the local businesses you rely on. Getting involved is a great way to have a say in issues that matter to you.

and how your teachers are certified and trained. States also levy taxes and control much business and environmental regulation. Local governments can also set minimum wages higher than the federally mandated minimum. As you can see, local politics is important. On top of that, the local level is where many national issues and national candidates get started. Politicians don't spring fully formed on the Senate floor. They start where they live—where you live. Changes at the local level often lead to changes at the national level. Except for foreign policy, almost everything the federal government does has a counterpart at the local level. If you have any interest at all in politics, you should take the time to learn about and get involved with local issues.

Fortunately, it can often be easier to cope with local political disagreements than with national ones. That doesn't mean local politics doesn't get nasty sometimes. Because local politics affect us so immediately and so close to home, we can get very passionate about them. Still, it's much easier to find common ground with your neighbors than with people all over the nation. Getting involved in local politics is also excellent practice for learning how to listen to people with different views and make compromises that work for everyone. National politics often seems like different interest groups arguing about abstract policy proposals. Local

Local meetings about local issues are more likely to end in agreement and even the start of new friendships than are national campaigns.

politics is often neighbors sitting down around the table to discuss the situation just outside the door. Whereas the changes made at the national level can sometimes take years to reach your neighborhood, local changes can have an immediate impact. Differences of opinion are just as real at the local level. But discussions at this level are often more likely to end in handshakes than insults.

Local politics is also more open to young people who want to get involved. Young people can take part in local politics, not just read about it in the news and argue about it on social media. In some areas, it can be difficult to get information about local issues. Sadly, many local newspapers are going out of business. But most cities have at least some coverage on the web. If you're interested, you can find out what's going on in your neighborhood, city, and state. Sometimes, the best way to do this is in person. You can attend neighborhood meetings and city council meetings. You can visit your local representatives. If you write or email your local representatives, there's a good chance you'll get a personal response. If you ask them to speak at an event at your school, you just might get a yes. If you've ever felt that you had no idea what the government is up to, you just need to start thinking locally. Getting informed about local matters helps you become a better citizen at every level of government. And it's great practice for learning how to disagree and still get along.

Home Ground Is Common Ground

Often, organizations that disagree about national issues find that they have much more in common locally. A

Working on local issues and problems with friends and neighbors is a great way to get a deeper understanding of the opposing viewpoint.

women's shelter might be in favor of a woman's right to decide whether to have an abortion. A Christian mission might be totally opposed to abortion. Both groups, however, are dedicated to helping women who are homeless or have been abused by their spouse. These groups can put aside their differences in the interest of helping the real people—their neighbors—

73

whom they see every day. Working closely together on local issues helps people with differing views come to know each other better. They may not agree on the issues, but they have a much deeper understanding of why other people support the positions they do.

People who work with local groups and organizations are reminded daily that their political opponents are their friends and neighbors. They understand far better than politicians in Washington, DC, or Ottawa, Canada, what life is like in their neighborhoods. They may still disagree mightily on plenty of issues. They do, however, have a much better idea about how to work out those disagreements. At the national level, it's easy just to cut off groups you don't agree with. The National Rifle Association (NRA) doesn't have to sit down with the Coalition to Stop Gun Violence. The companies that support oil pipelines don't have to interact with the neighborhoods those pipelines pass through. But at the local level, we have no choice. We live together. It's in cities and towns that Black Lives Matter activists and police officers sit down to talk. In cities and towns, parents who are worried about the number of guns on the street can talk one-on-one with hunters who worry that gun restrictions will keep them from being able to enjoy their sport.

Getting involved in local politics puts you right in the thick of the issues. You not only know far more about the issues, you know the people the issues affect. This doesn't mean everyone will agree. It does mean you can have real conversations with real people. And it means you are far more likely to understand one another. The more people understand one another, the easier it is to compromise. Getting involved in local politics doesn't mean increasing your opportunities

Putting Aside Politics for the Common Good

Often, young people are the first to put aside political differences. In 2017 Americans were suffering through some particularly difficult political disagreements. One of the most painful issues at that time concerned immigration. How many immigrants should the United States allow to settle within its borders? Should the number of immigrants from Muslim countries be limited? Questions like these were dividing the population. However, at the FIRST Global Challenge, an international robotics competition held in Washington, DC, there was no rancor. (FIRST is a program designed to inspire young people to be technology leaders and innovators.) Teens from 157 nations gathered to cheer on the

(continued on the next page)

(continued from the previous page)

competitors. The cheering was especially strong for Team Hope—a team made up of Syrian refugees. During the competition, teens from many nations— sometimes nations that were longtime enemies— formed friendships. Politics were put aside in the interest of science. And in the process, friendships began to matter more than politics. According to a news report, a member of Team Iran said, "Please

This Afghan all-girls robotics team prepares for the FIRST Global Challenge robotics competitions in July 2017, in Washington, DC.

see us today, we Israelis and Iranians were together and happy."

The organization's founder said that he hoped the kids who take part in FIRST programs will put aside politics to solve the world's most urgent problems— that can only be done by working together. Politics is an unavoidable topic. Bitterness and hatred are not. Teens may just be the ones to demonstrate this.

for conflict. It can mean plenty of opportunities for learning to get along in spite of those conflicts.

With Bowed Head

There was a time when churches stayed out of politics. Some still do. But more and more religious organizations are speaking out about political issues. This can be extremely difficult for people who are deeply religious yet don't agree with all of the positions of their church. It can be especially troubling when you don't see eye-to-eye with your church on political matters. It can be even harder to disagree with your minister, rabbi, or imam than with your mom or dad. Disagreeing with your religious leaders, however, doesn't mean you have to give up religion or even change your religious home.

The late paleontologist and developer of the idea of NOMA, Stephen Jay Gould, shown here in Paris in May 1991.

The late biologist Stephen Jay Gould proposed a concept he called "non-overlapping magisteria," or NOMA. Gould's suggestion was that religion and science have two different areas they are best suited for. Religion is best at dealing with spiritual matters. Science is best in matters of the physical world. Issues like climate change, for example, fall within the purview of science. Questions of whether there is a God—and if so, what that God might be like—come under the scope of religion. Gould's NOMA proposal was for eliminating conflicts between science and religion. But we can apply the general spirit of the idea to religion and politics. Basically, a person can believe in the tenets of her faith and still have political views that differ from those of her church. This does not mean that a religious organization should not take a position on political matters. It does mean that your participation in your faith does not have to depend on

End of Service

Americans are becoming less religious. A survey released in 2017 found that 24 percent of adult Americans and 38 percent of young adults are religiously unaffiliated. This means that they

(continued on the next page)

(continued from the previous page)

do not identify with and are not members of any organized religious group. Most people who identify as "religiously unaffiliated" consider themselves "secular." This does not mean that they do not have personal beliefs about matters Gould would place under the magisteria of religion. It just means that they are not members of any particular faith group. People who are religiously unaffiliated still have ethics. They are often quite active in charities and dedicated to a variety of social causes.

The United States is also becoming much more religiously diverse. In twenty states no single religious group has a greater share of the population than the religiously unaffiliated. Buddhists, Muslims, and Hindus are making up an increasing percentage of the US population. It remains to be seen how this will affect political discussions. It will certainly bring more points of view to the table for discussion.

your political views. And what better place to work out these differences than in a faith community? No matter the political differences, a faith community is a kind of family. Political differences should not tear it apart.

When it comes to disagreeing, how do you do it? The same guidelines for political disagreements with friends and family apply to those with faith families and faith leaders. Remember to be respectful of the opinions of others, listen, ask questions, and be kind. In addition, clergy can be very helpful when it comes to learning how to deal with friends and family members you disagree with. Living peacefully together in the world is a primary goal of most religions. Your faith leaders could be a great resource for working out political conflicts at home, at school, and in the community.

CHAPTER SIX

Online

Years ago, when people wondered what the twenty-first century might be like, they predicted robots, cell phones, and flying cars. They did not predict the innovation that would change the world most dramatically: social media. Chat rooms, Listservs, and live journals had been around for a long time. But the world of social media really took off in the early 2000s with Friendster, MySpace, and soon after that, Facebook and Twitter. As of 2017, 81 percent of the US population had a social media profile. In 2017, more than 60 percent of Canadians were on social media. Thanks to social media, the way people interact with each other, the way they celebrate birthdays and weddings, what they do on vacations, and how they play with their pets would all change. So would the way they discuss politics and elect presidents.

The Good and the Bad

Social media gets a lot of criticism. People check Facebook almost compulsively. They post to

Social media has made the world a smaller place. If we use it wisely, it can be a force for good.

Twitter and Instagram silly and insignificant things like videos of their cats and pictures of what they ate for lunch. They ignore people who are sitting next to them while they read a post from someone they don't even know.

But social media has it good points, too. Facebook has made it easy for friends and family to stay in touch, even when they live miles apart. People can get to know a much more diverse group of friends online than they can in person. It's easy to have Facebook friends all over the world. (And it's a great way to learn other languages.) People can share information with each other by social media. Sometimes, that's very important information. During hurricanes, governments use Twitter to keep people informed about the path and progress of big storms. During the dramatic 2017 hurricane season, people used social media (and text messaging) to keep each other posted about the best routes out of town and the availability of shelters, as well as to give information and directions to rescue workers.

When it comes to politics online, things get a little more complicated. All too often, they also get nasty.

Part of the problem is that social media is not well suited to political discourse. It's great for sharing jokes and slogans or for putting up the cyber equivalent of bumper stickers and campaign posters. It's not so great for reasoned discussions. You can't actually listen to someone on social media—you just trade opinions. Of course, many people share news and insightful articles, but that can be part of the problem. Social media is not the best place to get news.

When we're on social media, it can seem like

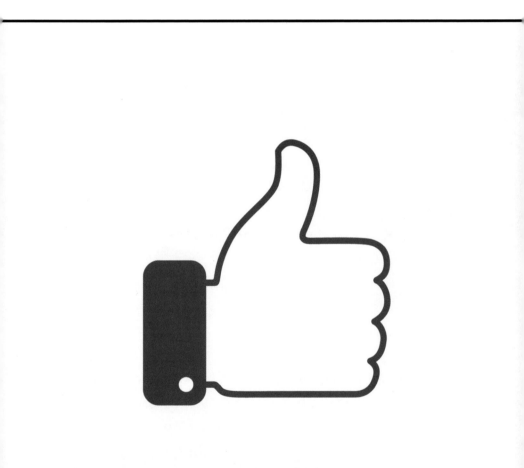

If you let it, Facebook's little Like button can have a disturbing amount of control over what parts of the world you see—and what you don't.

we're out in the middle of the world. But we might be in a much more sheltered place than we realize. On Facebook, not everything our friends post and not all posts by pages we follow show up in our feeds. This is a good thing. If everything were posted on our news feeds, we might starve to death before we got through reading it all. However, what does and does not appear is not random. Facebook decides, based on a complex and largely secret formula, what we are most likely to respond to, "like," or "share." Facebook is more likely to show liberal posts to people who are liberal leaning. People who lean conservative see more conservative-slanted posts. This includes news articles. It might feel nice and cozy to see only news you already agree with, but it's a lousy way to stay informed. (As of early 2018, Twitter shows every post by people you follow.)

You may ask what this has to do with political disagreements. After all, if we see only posts we agree with, we aren't likely to get into arguments. However, when something does get through that gets our ire up, or when we have discussions anywhere other than social media, we may be so badly misinformed that we aren't ready to have a conversation at all, much less a civil one. If you want to have healthy political exchanges on social media, you need to get your news from traditional sources.

Whom Can You Trust?

Staying well informed about politics can take a little savvy. Here are a few tips for navigating the web without being misled:

- Text written in all caps with lots of exclamation points is a sign that the site might not be legitimate news. Real, professional news articles will not be written that way. Also beware of articles that have words misspelled and poor grammar.

- Check the "About" page of any sites you suspect may be dodgy. See who is writing for and supporting the site. If the site isn't willing to tell you who pays the bills and writes its stories, then you shouldn't trust what it has to say.

- If the headline sounds a little bit outrageous, do some checking. Headlines like "MP Caught Selling Drugs to Kindergartners" or "Surgeon General Says US President Is Certifiably Insane" might just be "clickbait"—outrageous claims designed to get you to click on a link. Before clicking, Google the keywords of the story and see if reputable sites are covering it.

- The mainstream media is not flawless, but

(continued on the next page)

(continued from the previous page)

it is by far the best place to get your news. Mainstream outlets have fact checkers and are held accountable by the public. Find a few reputable sources of news and get your headlines there.

- Always double-check any news item before you share it on social media. You don't want to be responsible for spreading lies and nonsense.

A British journalist reads a fake news story on a website in March 2017. Learning to recognize the real from the fake is an important skill in a democracy.

Keeping It Casual

You might get the impression that it's impossible to avoid politics on social media. But you can do it if you try. Your social media accounts are yours—you can set the tone. Some people post a statement that very nicely explains their positions, such as "I love all my Facebook friends, but I don't love political arguments. Please don't be offended if I ignore or remove political posts. I'll talk to you all day about books, movies, and your family and pets. But count me out of politics."

You can repost the message whenever necessary. But you don't have to explain this every time someone tags you with a political post. Just do what you said and ignore or delete it. Obviously, you can't avoid seeing what other people share on their pages, but you don't have to spend any time reading it. Scan down your feed for the things you are interested in and get on with your life.

If you want to use social media for political discussions, you certainly can. But if those discussions are going to be civil and worthwhile, you have to be a bit cautious. Keep in mind the basics for civil political discussions at home, at school, and in the community. The same guidelines apply in cyberspace: show respect, stay calm, be kind, and listen to what the other person is saying. Oddly, that is harder than it seems. When you're online, there is a temptation to just let fly. It's so easy to say online things you'd never say in person.

When it's just you and your computer, it can be awfully easy to hit Send before you really mean to.

Also, no one is going to interrupt you. You can type out all your anger and frustration and hit send. Take that, you moron! Oops!

To avoid those "Oops!" moments, keep in mind a few helpful social media hints:

- **Pause before posting.** It takes only a minute to reread your post and give it a little thought. Ask yourself a few questions before you hit the post button. "Do I really mean this?" "Is this the best way to say it?" "Will this cause any harm to me or anyone else?" Don't post until you are satisfied with your answers.

- **Never post anything you wouldn't say in person.** It's a lot easier to be snarky, even mean, when don't have to look at the person you're talking to. Stop and imagine this person. Pretend he or she is sitting right beside you. If you wouldn't say it in person, don't post it. It's also much easier to misunderstand people when you can't see them. When you're having a conversation online, you can't see the facial expressions, the eyes, or the body language of the people you're talking with. That makes it harder to know when they're joking and when they're serious. If you're not sure, give the person the benefit of the doubt. Many an argument has started and many a friendship ruined because someone took a post the wrong way and responded to what he thought he heard, rather than what was intended.

Flip-Flops: Totally Appropriate Footwear

Politicians catch a lot of grief when they change their positions on the issues. People accuse them of flip-flopping and hint that maybe they can't be trusted. It can be difficult to know why politicians change their views. They might change their positions just because they think they'll get more votes. Or they might change their positions because that will attract more donations to their campaigns. Or maybe their positions really have evolved.

Flip-flops aren't always bad. Not for politicians and especially not for the rest of us. When you carefully consider all the evidence, listen to a wide range of well-supported opinions, and give the issue a lot of thought, you well might change your mind. That's not only OK, it's smart. It's silly to stick to a position just because you don't want to look like you can't make up your mind. Just be sure that you base your opinions on solid facts and reason, then wear those flip-flops proudly.

- **Never be a bully.** Being discourteous and unkind is bad enough. Being a bully is even worse. And it's all too easy to do online. It's especially easy to do when lots of other people are jumping in and jumping on someone. But bullying can ruin a life. Just don't do it.

They're Coming for Me!

Ok, so you've decided to keep your posts civil. But what about everyone else? What do you do when someone attacks you online? Some people have thought they were being the nicest, gentlest people on social media, only to discover that they've set off a firestorm. Say you see a story about a couple adopting a special-needs baby. How sweet! You repost it thinking it's just a feel-good story. Then some of your friends start criticizing you because the couple was gay. Or maybe in your post you used a term that you didn't realize could be offensive to some people. You were just trying to share something sweet, but now you've got all this controversy on your Facebook page. You can ignore it all. But you don't want people to think you meant to do harm by using an offensive term. And you feel the need to defend the gay parents who are being treated so harshly right there on your page! You'd like to totally stay out of this kind of thing, but you can't. You just stepped right in it. This is when you need a get-out-quick strategy. It's

Remember, when things get too rough online, you really can just walk away. The real world is still a pretty fine place (and you can get back online later).

simple enough. First remove all offensive posts from your page. Apologize publicly if you've said anything you regret. And make a simple statement supporting the people who've been insulted on your page. Then let it go and move on to something else.

It's never too late to stop an online discussion that has gotten out of hand. You can just say, "I'm not comfortable with the tone of this conversation. Let's talk again later about something less confrontational." Then sign off and do something else. It may seem as if you have to defend every point and straighten out every mistake. You really don't. Internet conversations dry up like morning fog. Soon, everyone will be talking about something else. When things get too hot online, you can just take a break. The virtual world will still be there when you get back—and the craziness may be over by then. And if it's not, it's almost certain to be a different craziness.

You don't have to give up life online to keep political discussions civil. You don't even have to give up talking about politics online. But keeping things civil online does take a little extra effort.

Maintaining good relationships with friends and family doesn't have to mean giving up politics. It just requires that we be truly civil.

Glossary

civil Relating to citizens and their role in government (as opposed to military); also, courteous and polite.

coalition A temporary coming together of different groups for a shared purpose.

congenial Pleasant, agreeable.

democracy A form of government in which the ultimate authority rests with the people.

discourse Discussion or exchange of ideas.

Electoral College The group of people who, as per instructions from their states, elect the president of the United States.

ethics A set of moral principles; a framework for making moral decisions.

evolve Gradually change over time.

federal Having to do with or relating to the central government in a system in which government is made up of a union of smaller governments.

hoax A trick or deception, usually with malicious intent.

homogeneous A group or substance whose parts are all of the same or similar kind.

ire Anger that is usually strong and shown out in the open.

LGBTQ An initialism that stands for "lesbian, gay, bisexual, transgender, and queer."

magisteria (plural of magisterium) The teaching authority of a religious body, especially the Catholic Church.

ovation Applause or a similar demonstration of appreciation.

polarize To split into separate and often nearly opposite factions or groups.

rancor Bitterness or ill will.

spectrum A range of something (such as political opinions).

tenet A belief or political or philosophical position.

vivisection The practice of operating on live animals for research.

xenophobia Fear or hatred of people from other countries.

Boys and Girls Clubs of America
1275 Peachtree St. NE
Atlanta, GA 30309-3506
(404) 487-5700
Email: Info@BGCA.org
Website: http://bca.org
Facebook: @bgca.clubs
Twitter and Instagram: @bcga_clubs
A nationwide organization that offers many after-
    school activities, including ones that encourage
    young people to become kind, caring, and
    responsible citizens.

Canadian Civil Liberties Association
90 Eglinton Avenue East
Toronto, ON M4P 2Y3
Canada
(416) 363-0321
Email: mail@ccla.org
Website: https://ccla.org
Facebook and Twitter: @cancivlib
An organization that fights for the civil liberties,
    human rights, and democratic freedoms of
    people all across Canada.

Media Smarts: Canada's Centre for Digital and
    Media Literacy
205 Catherine Street, Suite 100

Ottawa, ON K2P 1C3
Canada
(613) 224-7721
Email: Info@mediasmarts.ca
Website: http://mediasmarts.ca
Facebook and Twitter: @MediaSmarts
An organization dedicated to ensuring that
children and youth have the critical-thinking
skills necessary to engage with media as active
and informed digital citizens.

Teaching Tolerance
400 Washington Avenue
Montgomery, AL 36104
(888) 414-7752
Website: https://www.splcenter.org/teaching
-tolerance
Facebook: @SPLCenter
Twitter: @splcenter
A project of the Southern Poverty Law Center,
this group is dedicated to combating
prejudice among youth and promoting
equality, inclusiveness, and equitable learning
environments in the classroom.

Young America's Foundation
11480 Commerce Park Drive, Suite 600
Reston, VA 20191
(703) 318-9608

Send email through online contact form.
Website: http://www.yaf.org
Facebook: @youngamericasfoundation
Twitter: @yaf
An organization dedicated to making sure young Americans understand the principles of conservatism: individual freedom, a strong national defense, free enterprise, and traditional values.

Young Democrats of America
PO Box 77496
Washington, DC 20013-8496
Contact via website contact page.
Website: https://www.yda.org
Facebook and Twitter: @youngdems
The official youth arm of the Democratic Party, this group aims to encourage youth to participate in the political process, influence the ideals of the Democratic Party, and support progressive issues.

For Further Reading

Alfirenka, Caitlin, and Martin Gandor. *I Will Always Write Back: How One Letter Changed Two Lives.* With Liz Welch. New York, NY: Little, Brown, 2015.

Cain, Susan. *Quiet Power: The Secret Strengths of Introverted Kids.* New York, NY: Puffin, 2016.

Conrad, Jessamyn. *What You Should Know About Politics ... but Don't: A Non-partisan Guide to the Issues That Matter.* New York, NY: Arcade, 2016.

Donovan, Sandy. *Communication Smarts: How to Express Yourself Best in Conversations, Texts, E-Mails, and More.* Minneapolis, MN: Twenty-First Century Books, 2013.

Fleischer, Jeff. *Votes of Confidence: A Young Person's Guide to American Elections.* San Francisco, CA: Zest, 2018.

Gitlin, Martin, ed. *When Is Free Speech Hate Speech?* New York, NY: Greenhaven, 2018.

Le Guin, Ursula. *Voices.* Boston, MA: Houghton Mifflin Harcourt, 2006.

Mapua, Jeff. *Coping with Cyberbullying.* New York, NY: Rosen Publishing, 2018.

McKee, Jonathan. *The Teens Guide to Social Media . . . and Mobile Devices: 21 Tips to Wise Posting in an Insecure World.* Uhrichsville, OH: Shiloh Run Press, 2017.

Petrikowski, Nicki Peter. *Working for Tolerance and Social Change Through Service Learning.* New York: Rosen Publishing, 2015.

Sears, Kathleen. *American Government 101: From the Continental Congress to the Iowa Caucus, Everything You Need to Know About US Politics.* Avon, MA: Adams Media, 2016.

Skeen, Michelle, et al. *Communications Skills for Teens: How to Listen, Express, and Connect for Success.* Oakland, CA: New Harbinger, 2016.

Bibliography

Alwin, Duane, et al. *Political Attitudes over the Lifespan: The Bennington Women After Fifty Years.* Madison, WI: University of Wisconsin Press, 1992.

Carmon, Irin. "What Made the Friendship Between Scalia and Ginsburg Work?" *Washington Post*, February 13, 2016. https://www.washingtonpost.com/posteverything/wp/2016/02/13/what-made-scalia-and-ginsburgs-friendship-work/?utm_term=.ed21bfbca7cc.

Carville, James, and Mary Matalin. *Love and War: Twenty Years. Three Presidents, Two Daughters, and One Louisiana Home.* New York, NY: Blue Rider, 2014.

Desilver, Drew. "The Politics of American Generations: How Age Affects Attitude and Voting Behavior." Pew Research Center, July 9, 2014. http://www.pewresearch.org/fact-tank/2014/07/09/the-politics-of-american-generations-how-age-affects-attitudes-and-voting-behavior.

Frost, Robert. *The Poetry of Robert Frost.* Edited by Edward Connery Lathem. New York, NY: Henry Holt, 1975.

Ghitza, Yair, and Andrew Gelman. "The Great Society, Reagan's Revolution, and Generations of Presidential Voting." Columbia University, June 2014. http://www.stat.columbia

.edu/~gelman/research/unpublished/cohort _voting_20140605.pdf.

Gilbert, Sophie. "*Teen Vogue's* Political Coverage Isn't Surprising." *Atlantic*, December 12, 2016. https://www.theatlantic.com/entertainment /archive/2016/12/teen-vogue-politics/510374.

Gould, Stephen Jay. *The Richness of Life: The Essential Stephen Jay Gould.* Edited by Steven Rose. New York, NY: Norton, 2007.

Gross, Rachel E. "Turns Out Your Kids Are Not Receptacles for Your Political Beliefs." Slate, November 19, 2015. http://www.slate.com /blogs/the_slatest/2015/11/19/study_kids _aren_t_accepting_parental_politics_as_we _thought.html.

Hersh, Eitan. "How Many Republicans Marry Democrats?" FiveThirtyEight, June 28, 2016. https://fivethirtyeight.com/features/how -many-republicans-marry-democrats.

Hohmann, James. "Daily 202: McCain and Kerry Outline Lessons from Vietnam After Watching New Ken Burns Documentary." *Washington Post*, September 13, 2017. https://www .washingtonpost.com/news/powerpost /paloma/daily-202/2017/09/13/daily-202 -mccain-and-kerry-outline-lessons-from -vietnam-after-watching-new-ken-burns -documentary/59b86be930fb045176650c33.

Kenworthy, Josh. "Teachers' New Catch 22: Students Want to Talk Politics, but Their Parents Don't." *Christian Science Monitor*, March 13, 2017. https://www.csmonitor.com /EqualEd/2017/0313/Teachers-new-Catch -22-Students-want-to-talk-politics-but-their -parents-don-t.

McKibben, Sarah. "Using Fishbowls to Talk Politics." ASCD InService, October 26, 2015. http://inservice.ascd.org/using-fishbowls-to -talk-politics.

NPR Staff. "Ginsburg and Scalia: Best Buddies." NPR, February 15, 2016. http://www.npr .org/2016/02/15/466848775/scalia-ginsburg -opera-commemorates-sparring-supreme -court-friendship.

Talisse, Robert B. "Democracy Is Like Fun: You Can't Set Your Mind to Having It." Aeon, October 6, 2017. https://aeon.co/ideas/democracy-is -like-fun-you-cant-set-your-mind-to-having -it?utm_source=Aeon+Newsletter&utm _campaign=fcd6982175.

Index

About the Author

Avery Elizabeth Hurt is the author of numerous books for children and young adults, including the Rosen title *Coping with Hate and Intolerance*. She has friends and relatives all across the political spectrum and is happy to say that so far no one has actually thrown the Thanksgiving turkey at anyone else.

Photo Credits

Cover sirtravelalot/Shutterstock.com; p. 5 AntonioGuillem/iStock/Thinkstock; pp. 8–9, 16–17 Klaus Vedfelt/DigitalVision/Getty Images; pp. 14–15 lathuric/E+/Getty Images; p. 20 Hero Images/Getty Images; p. 23 vectorfusionart/Shutterstock.com; p. 27 © iStockphoto.comKatarzynaBialasiewicz; p. 28 © iStockphoto.com/CreativeI; p. 30 Monkey Business Images/Thinkstock; p. 33 5 second Studio/Shutterstock.com; pp. 38–39 Erika Goldring/Getty Images; p. 43 BananaStock/Thinkstock; pp. 48–49 Image Source/Getty Images; pp. 50–51 Peter Glass/Stockbyte/Getty Images; p. 53 DMEPhotography/iStock/Thinkstock; p. 55 Photodisc/Thinkstock; p. 58 MCT/Tribune News Service/Getty Images; p. 60 Dominick Reuter/AFP/Getty Images; p. 63 MangoStar_Studio/iStock/Thinkstock; p. 69 Jetta Productions/Blend Images/Getty Images; p. 71 Thomas Barwick/DigitalVision/Getty Images; p. 73 Thomas Barwick/Stone/Getty Images; p. 76 Paul J. Richards/AFP/Getty Images; p. 78 Ulf Andersen/Hulton Archive/Getty Images; p. 83 Bloomicon/Shutterstock.com; p. 85 BARS graphics/Shutterstock.com; p. 88 Daniel Sorabji/AFP/Getty Images; p. 90 arek_malang/Shutterstock.com; pp. 94–95 © iStockphoto.com/MarioGuti.

Design and Layout: Nicole Russo-Duca; Editor and Photo Researcher: Heather Moore Niver